# Cheeky Chinchillas

**Kelly Doudna**
AUTHOR

**C.A. Nobens**
ILLUSTRATOR

Consulting Editor, Diane Craig, M.A./Reading Specialist

A Division of ABDO

ABDO
Publishing Company

# visit us at www.abdopublishing.com

Published by ABDO Publishing Company, a division of ABDO, P.O. Box 398166, Minneapolis, Minnesota 55439. Copyright © 2013 by Abdo Consulting Group, Inc. International copyrights reserved in all countries. No part of this book may be reproduced in any form without written permission from the publisher. SandCastle™ is a trademark and logo of ABDO Publishing Company.

Printed in the United States of America, North Mankato, Minnesota
102012
012013

 PRINTED ON RECYCLED PAPER

Editor: Liz Salzmann
Content Developer: Nancy Tuminelly
Cover and Interior Design and Production: Kelly Doudna, Mighty Media, Inc.
Photo Credits: Shutterstock, ThinkStock

**Library of Congress Cataloging-in-Publication Data**

Doudna, Kelly, 1963-
  Cheeky chinchillas / by Kelly Doudna ; illustrator C.A. Nobens.
     p. cm. -- (Unusual pets)
  ISBN 978-1-61783-398-4
  1. Chinchillas as pets--Juvenile literature. I. Nobens, C. A., ill. II. Title.
  SF459.C48D68 2013
  636.935'93--dc23
                              2011050725

**SandCastle™ Level:** Transitional

SandCastle™ books are created by a team of professional educators, reading specialists, and content developers around five essential components—phonemic awareness, phonics, vocabulary, text comprehension, and fluency—to assist young readers as they develop reading skills and strategies and increase their general knowledge. All books are written, reviewed, and leveled for guided reading, early reading intervention, and Accelerated Reader® programs for use in shared, guided, and independent reading and writing activities to support a balanced approach to literacy instruction. The SandCastle™ series has four levels that correspond to early literacy development. The levels are provided to help teachers and parents select appropriate books for young readers.

Emerging Readers
(no flags)

Beginning Readers
(1 flag)

Transitional Readers
(2 flags)

Fluent Readers
(3 flags)

# Contents

# Unusual Pets

Unusual pets can be interesting and fun! Unusual pets might also eat unusual food. They might have special care needs. It is a good idea to learn about your new friend before bringing it home.

There are special laws for many unusual animals. Make sure the kind of pet you want is allowed in your city and state.

# Chinchilla Basics

Type of animal

Chinchillas are **mammals**.

Adult weight

1 to 2 pounds (.5 to 1 kg)

Life expectancy

10 to 20 years

Natural habitat

Andes Mountains
in South America

Nick has a pet chinchilla. He likes to hold it. It has soft fur.

Chinchillas have very thick fur. They roll around in dust to clean their fur.

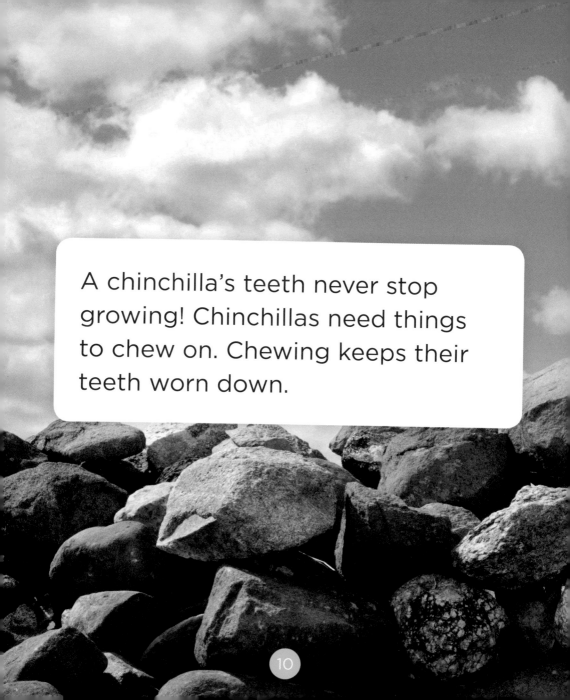

A chinchilla's teeth never stop growing! Chinchillas need things to chew on. Chewing keeps their teeth worn down.

Chinchillas are friendly. But they like to be alone sometimes. They need places where they can hide.

# A Chinchilla Story

Willa and her mother
visit an animal **shelter**.
They see a gray chinchilla.
They smile at each other.
"She's perfect!" says Willa.
"I'll name her Vanilla."

Willa gives Vanilla

a box where she can sleep.

Vanilla curls into a ball.

She doesn't make a peep.

She sleeps almost all day.

Then she wakes up ready to play.

Vanilla runs around.

Willa watches her climb.

Vanilla **scampers** and jumps.

She makes Willa smile.

Then Vanilla quiets down.

She sits with Willa for a while.

Willa and her chinchilla
have fun all the time.
Willa kisses Vanilla's nose.
She gives her a big hug.
She says, "Vanilla,
I'm glad you're mine!"

# Fun Facts

* The sea otter is the only animal with **denser** fur than a chinchilla.

* Chinchillas can't sweat.

* The chinchilla is named after the Chincha people of the Andes Mountains in South America.

* People who are **allergic** to dogs and cats often are not allergic to chinchillas.

# Chinchilla Quiz

Read each sentence below. Then decide whether it is true or false!

1. Chinchillas have soft fur.

2. A chinchilla will roll in dust to clean its fur.

3. Willa gets Vanilla at a pet store.

4. Vanilla sleeps in a wooden basket.

5. Vanilla jumps and **scampers**.

# Glossary

**allergic** – unable to touch, breathe, or eat certain things without getting sick.

**dense** – thick or crowded together.

**mammal** – a warm-blooded animal that has hair and whose females produce milk to feed their young.

**scamper** – to run in a playful way.

**shelter** – a place where people or animals who are hurt or need a home can stay.